Home Evenings
for *Newlyweds*

Home Evenings
for *Newlyweds*

WALNUT SPRINGS PRESS

Walnut Springs Press
4110 South Highland Drive
Salt Lake City, Utah 84124

Printed in the United States of America

ISBN: 978-1-59992-946-0

Contents

Introduction   7

His Life   9

Not as the World Seeth   11

The Small and Simple Things   13

Prepare the Way   15

Everything Good   17

Talents   20

Blessed Are They   22

Trust in the Lord   24

The Song of the Heart   26

The Atonement   28

The Sacrament   29

Two on the Road to Emmaus   31

Where Can I Turn for Peace?   33

Becoming Like Him   35

Becoming   37

Gratitude   39

Agency   41

Prayer   43

Scriptures   45

Knowledge   47

Temperance   48

Diligence   51

Covenants   54

Service   56

Hope   58

Faith   60

Charity   62

Humility   64

Virtue	66
Light	68
Prove Me	69
His Work and His Glory	71
Pre-Earth Life	73
Earth as a Witness	75
One Flesh	77
Revelation	78
Cease to Be Idle	79
Prophets	81
General Conference	83
Priesthood and the Family	84
Creating	86
Zion	87
Trials	89
Stand Still	92
Family History: Temple Work	94
Family History: Stories	97
Missionary Work	99
Come and See	101
Angels Are Near You	103
Centered on Him	105
Valentine's Day	107
Easter	110
Memorial Day	112
Fourth of July	114
Thanksgiving	115
Christmas	117
Dessert Ideas	121
About the Author	127

Introduction

Our first family nights as a newly married couple were difficult for my husband and me. We spent so much time together that Monday nights often felt like just another evening. How could we have lessons for two, and what should the lessons be about?

If you and your spouse have asked those same questions, this book is for you. It is packed full of fun activities for newlyweds, with lessons that encourage gospel discussion and learning. The fifty-two lessons can be done in any order, with the last six designed for holidays. Many of the lessons include alternate ideas for activities that could be incorporated into additional family nights.

Each lesson focuses on an aspect of Jesus Christ's life, character, or work. I have realized that as my husband and I center our lives on Jesus Christ, we find guidance for whatever we face. I hope these lessons help you and your spouse come to know the Savior better.

P.S. See the dessert ideas and recipes at the end of the book. Every family night deserves a treat!

His Life

Not as the World Seeth

Preparation

You will need a camera and a way to view the photos.

Song

"The Lord Is My Light" (*Hymns*, no. 89)

Lesson

Take close-up photos of common objects outdoors or in your home. Don't let your spouse see what you are photographing. Once you each have three or four pictures, have him or her guess what each one is. Read 1 Samuel 16:7. The Lord tells us He sees things that man does not see. As with the photos, sometimes we don't realize what something truly is because of our limited view.

Read Luke 2:25–38. Consider how many people must have been in the temple that day. Only a few realized the significance of the humble couple with the small baby. Here was the Son of God, yet so many temple-goers walked right by. What was different about Simeon and Anna that allowed them to see and recognize the Savior?

Simeon said that Christ would be "A light to lighten the gentiles." Read Doctrine and Covenants 45:7. Jesus Christ is the Light of the World. He lights the darkness around us, yet so many go about life not seeing Him. What can you do to make sure you see the Light like Simeon and Anna? How is being able to see and recognize the Savior's light a blessing? How can it change how you view others?

Additional Resources

Dieter F. Uchtdorf, "Receiving a Testimony of Light and Truth," General Conference, Oct. 2014 (lds.org/general-conference/2014/10/receiving-a-testimony-of-light-and-truth).

Marion G. Romney, "The Light Shineth," General Conference, Oct. 1971 (lds.org/general-conference/1971/10/the-light-shineth).

Thomas S. Monson, "Yellow Canaries with Gray on Their Wings," General Conference, Apr. 1973 (lds.org/general-conference/1973/04/yellow-canaries-with-gray-on-their-wings).

By Small and Simple Things

Preparation

For this lesson and activity, you will need bread and at least two of your preferred sandwich fillings. For example: peanut butter and jelly, cheese and a deli meat, lettuce and tomatoes, and so on. Put all the ingredients for your sandwiches in a container, along with any utensils you might need for spreading or cutting. Spread out a picnic blanket where you will have your FHE.

Song

"As I Search the Holy Scriptures" (*Hymns*, no. 277)

Lesson

Sit on your picnic blanket with the container of supplies within reach. Read Luke 2:40, 52, and Doctrine and Covenants 93:11–13. What do these verses teach us about how Jesus Christ grew and learned? Read Doctrine and Covenants 93:19–20. What do we need to do to receive a fullness of the Father? Sometimes keeping the commandments can seem too simple and too small. Sometimes we over look the small things Heavenly Father asks us to do.

Now it is time to make your sandwich. Since people do things at different times of day, use yesterday as a guide when thinking about the following questions.

Read 3 Nephi 18:21. If you prayed together yesterday, take a slice of bread. Read Matthew 6:6. If you said personal prayers morning and night yesterday, take a slice of bread.

Read John 5:39. If you read your scriptures yesterday as a couple, put one filling on your sandwich. If you read your scriptures personally, add another filling. For more fillings, consider things we are commanded to do daily or weekly. Just as simple ingredients combine to make a sandwich, keeping the commandments—no matter how small or simple they seem—allows us to grow and learn, grace for grace, day by day until we can receive all the Lord has promised us.

Read Doctrine and Covenants 63:23. The more we learn and grow through keeping the commandments, the more we allow the Savior and His gospel to enrich our lives. Commit to pray and study the scriptures daily as a couple. If these things are not already part of your routine, schedule them at a time that will work for both of you.

Enjoy your simple picnic together.

Additional Resources

Linda S. Reeves, "Protection from Pornography—a Christ-Focused Home," General Conference, Apr. 2014 (lds.org/general-conference/2014/04/protection-from-pornography-a-christ-focused-home).

Dieter F. Uchtdorf, "Of Things That Matter Most," General Conference, Oct. 2010 (lds.org/general-conference/2010/10/of-things-that-matter-most).

Prepare the Way

Preparation

Gather the ingredients for a meal that can be prepared ahead of time. Some examples might be lasagna, a rice casserole, a stir-fry, or a slow-cooker meal. If you don't know what to make, do an internet search for "prepare-ahead meals."

Song

"Today While the Sun Shines" (*Hymns*, no. 229)

Lesson

What are some things you prepare for? (Examples might be your job, meals, the temple, and so on.) Have you ever had something important happen that you weren't prepared for? How did that experience compare to times when you were prepared?

Read Matthew 3:1–10. John the Baptist was sent to prepare the way for Jesus Christ. Why did Heavenly Father want to prepare people for the Savior's coming?

Heavenly Father has called us to prepare the way for Christ's Second Coming. Read Doctrine and Covenants 35:3–4, but put your own names in place of Sydney Rigdon's. Read Doctrine and Covenants 109:38, 46. How is our calling to prepare the way similar to the calling of John the Baptist? How does preparing ourselves first allow us to be an example to others? What promise does the Lord give to those who are prepared?

All the Savior's blessings and promises are available because He prepared the way for us. Although our own missions on earth may be daunting at times, we know we can trust in the Lord because He has already prepared for our trials. We learn a little of those preparations in Doctrine and Covenants 19:16–19. Read these verses together. Because of the Savior's preparations for us, we don't ever have to feel alone as we do as He commands us. Read 1 Nephi 17:13.

The Savior's preparation for the Atonement began with a simple step: baptism. As He obeyed the commandment to be baptized, He started on the path toward the sacrifice that would save us all. What steps can you take to fulfill your mission on earth? How does receiving ordinances and making covenants prepare you?

Prepare tomorrow's dinner tonight as a couple. Work together and have fun. Tomorrow all you have to do is add the finishing touches and enjoy a stress-free evening.

Additional Resources

For more scriptures about the Savior's preparations for us, see John 14:2, Ether 12:32–34, and Doctrine and Covenants 106:8.

Linda K. Burton, "Prepared in a Manner that Never Had Been Known," General Conference, Oct. 2014 (lds.org/general-conference/2014/10/prepared-in-a-manner-that-never-had-been-known).

Everything Good

Preparation

Access the Bible video *Jesus Forgives Sins and Heals a Man with Palsy* (lds.org/bible-videos/videos/jesus-forgives-sins-and-heals-a-man-stricken-with-palsy).

Song

"Improve the Shining Moments" (*Hymns,* no. 226)

Lesson

Read Acts 10:38. Are there times when you hesitate to help or do good? What keeps you from doing good or reaching out to others?

Watch *Jesus Forgives Sins and Heals a Man with Palsy.* Like so many of the people who sought out Jesus, the people who brought the man with palsy to Him didn't know how their efforts to help their friend would turn out. They came anyway. How were their efforts rewarded with good things? What might the crowd and onlookers have learned because of this event?

Sometimes we don't know how things will turn out. Sometimes we stumble or make mistakes. But God can always turn our efforts into good things. He has told us in Doctrine and Covenants 90:24 that if we "search diligently, pray always, and be believing . . . all things shall work together for [our] good."

Read Moroni 7:13. If everything good comes from God, then our good works become *His* work. Throughout His life, the Savior reached out to others and blessed their efforts to come to Him. It was not by accident or chance that He healed and blessed people. Likewise, our opportunities to love and serve are not by chance.

President Spencer W. Kimball taught: "We must remember that those mortals we meet in parking lots, offices, elevators, and elsewhere are that portion of mankind God has given us to love and to serve. It will do us little good to speak of the general brotherhood of mankind if we cannot regard those who are all around us as our brothers and sisters."[1]

Cut out the strips of paper on the following page and place them in a jar or container. For the next week or two, draw a service idea from the jar and do the service sometime during the day. You can use your own ideas, too.

---

1. Spencer W. Kimball, "Jesus the Perfect Leader," *Ensign,* Aug.1979 (lds.org/ensign/1979/08/jesus-the-perfect-leader).

Service Jar

Copy this list, cut it into strips, and put them in a jar.

Say hi to someone you don't know.

Write a kind message for someone.

Open a door for a stranger.

Do a household chore your spouse normally does.

Contact a friend you haven't spoken to in a long time.

Call your mom or dad.

Call a grandparent, aunt, uncle, cousin, or sibling.

Smile at someone you don't know.

Post a spiritual quote on a social media site.

Send your spouse an uplifting text message.

Say thank you to someone.

Give a sincere compliment.

Spend an evening doing something your spouse wants to do.

Give someone a flower or other simple gift.

Share your time, a talent, an umbrella, a meal, or a book you enjoyed.

Talents

Preparation

Find a basket, bucket, or box, and a ball for tossing. Prepare for the talent you and your spouse decide to learn (see the lesson for more information and ideas).

Song

"Come Let Us Anew" (*Hymns,* no. 217)

Lesson

Read Matthew 25:14–29. The Lord has blessed each of us with at least one talent. Read the following quote from Elder Robert C. Gay:

> *Some of you will say, "Who am I? I am no genius. I have no unique talent. I am nobody special. I just feel fortunate to get through each day." To each of you, no matter your fears or uncertainties, I say, 'Never sell yourself short!' . . .*
>
> *Let this one absolute truth from heaven sink into your mind and heart—you have the power within you to astonish this world. You are a son or daughter of the most powerful Being and force in the universe. You are endowed with His all-knowing light and truth, by which you may forsake all evil (see D&C 93:37). Moreover, the Lord teaches this profound*

truth: "To every man is given a gift by the Spirit of God" (D&C 46:11).[2]

Get your basket and ball (or a basketball and hoop). Toss the ball into the basket. If you don't make it, your spouse takes a turn. If you make it, your spouse has to shoot from the same place as you did. If your spouse misses, he or she gets a letter. For this version, spell out the word "talent." Every time you get a letter, you have to say one of your talents. The last person to get all the letters is the winner. Try moving the basket and shooting from different places.

Pick a talent you would like to develop. Tonight or in the coming week, work on that talent. You can have your spouse teach you something. There are also online resources that teach skills like dancing, crocheting, sewing, fixing or building something, or how to cook a new food. Many communities offer in-person classes for a small fee. Whatever skill you choose, learn it together and have fun.

Additional Resources

James E. Faust, "I Believe I Can, I Knew I Could," General Conference, Oct. 2002 (lds.org/general-conference/2002/10/i-believe-i-can-i-knew-i-could).

Gordon B. Hinckley, "The Light Within You," General Conference, Apr. 1995. (lds.org/general-conference/1995/04/the-light-within-you).

2. Robert C. Gay, "Your Journey of Giving," *Ensign,* Sept. 2013. (lds.org/ensign/2014/09/your-journey-of-giving).

Blessed Are They

Preparation

Get a pen and a notebook or sheet of paper.

Song

"Let Us Oft Speak Kind Words" (*Hymns*, no. 232)

Lesson

Search Matthew 5 through 7 for counsel that can apply to marriage relationships. With your pen, divide a sheet of paper into two columns. Label the first column "Matthew 5–7." List the things you found.

Read Ephesians 4. Label your second column "Ephesians 4," then list the counsel from this chapter that you can apply to your relationship. How can the principles taught by Jesus in the Sermon on the Mount, and by Paul to the Ephesians, help you and your spouse be more unified? In what ways do your differences allow you to work together in better and more efficient ways?

Consider holding family councils. You may want to schedule a monthly council, but they can also be called whenever a need arises. Discuss issues like goals, finances, major life choices, upcoming events, or things the family has accomplished. Remember to start with a prayer. Follow the counsel given in the scripture passages you just read as you interact with each other, keeping in mind a goal of unity between you, your spouse, and the Lord.

Additional Resources

Neal A. Maxwell, "'Repent of [Our] Selfishness' (D&C 56:8)," General Conference, Apr. 1999 (lds.org/general-conference/1999/04/repent-of-our-selfishness-d-c-56-8).

Richard G. Scott, "For Peace at Home," General Conference, Apr. 2013 (lds.org/general-conference/2013/04/for-peace-at-home).

Nicole Eck, "Counsel Together Oft: Family Councils for Couples," *Ensign*, Jan. 2015 (lds.org/ensign/2015/01/young-adults/counsel-together-oft-family-councils-for-couples).

Trust in the Lord

Preparation

Pick a local hiking area or outdoor trail to visit. Keep in mind your time schedule and how much physical activity you are used to. Wear good hiking shoes, and bring water, snacks, sunscreen, jackets, sunglasses, etc.

Song

"Lead, Kindly Light" (*Hymns*, no. 97)

Lesson

Before or during your hike, read Matthew 14:23–33 together. The Savior sent His disciples to cross the sea without Him. In the midst of their journey, winds arose and the waves grew large. Has the Spirit ever sent you somewhere unexpected? What challenges did you encounter along the way?

The disciples must have felt they were far from the reach and aid of Jesus, yet He came to them, walking on the very water that tossed them. How does knowing you are never too far from the Savior's reach help you when you face difficulties?

Peter sank because he began to doubt and fear. In what ways does doubt lead us to look away from the Savior and sink in our own troubles? Compare trusting in the Lord to following a trail on a hike. What would happen if you feared the trail wasn't going the right direction? What if you left the path, looking for a better way? Read Proverbs 3:5–6. Unlike trails that can have the wrong signs or be altered by the elements, Jesus Christ is never wrong and never changes. He always knows the right way and the best way.

Additional Resources

Richard G. Scott, "Trust in the Lord," General Conference, Oct. 1995 (lds.org/general-conference/1995/10/trust-in-the-lord).

Jeffrey R. Holland, "Lord, I Believe," General Conference, Apr. 2013 (lds.org/general-conference/2013/04/lord-i-believe).

The Song of the Heart

Preparation

Have your music-playing devices nearby.

Song

"I Need Thee Every Hour" (*Hymns*, no. 98)

Lesson

Think of times when you needed the Lord. How did you ask for His aid? Read Matthew 26:30. Jesus and His disciples sang a hymn before He went to the Garden of Gethsemane to suffer for our sins. How do you think singing the hymn might have prepared Him for what was to come? How might it have prepared the disciples?

Read Doctrine and Covenants 25:12. How does the Lord feel about music? What blessings has music brought into your life? Each spouse can share some of his or her experiences with music. If you have access to a song that has helped you, listen to it together. Music can be a part of our worship in "joy or pain." Read Doctrine and Covenants 136:28. How can you make uplifting music a bigger part of your life?

You and your spouse may have different musical preferences. Putting those differences aside, create a playlist of uplifting songs you can agree on. Make this your go-to playlist when you are together.

Consider making a special playlist for Sundays or other times when you need a more spiritual atmosphere. You may also want to set aside time to make personal playlists of uplifting songs. With these songs readily available, they can be a source of personal revelation and comfort, as well as joy and inspiration.

Lds.org provides many music resources. A few of interest may be:

- lds.org/music: includes access to lyrics and recordings of the music in *Hymns* and the *Children's Songbook.*
- lds.org/youth/music: listen to or download free uplifting songs used for seminary, institute, and EFY. There are even a few songs by popular LDS musicians.
- mormonchannel.org/how-to-listen/stream: live-stream uplifting music anytime you have internet access.
- lds.org/general-conference/music: download choir songs from general conference.

Additional Resources

Dallin H. Oaks, "Worship through Music," General Conference, Oct. 1994 (lds.org/general-conference/1994/10/worship-through-music).

The Atonement

Preparation

Access the video *Lifting Burdens* on lds.org (lds.org/media-library/video/2009-10-38-lifting-burdens). Have a timer or stopwatch nearby, and a pen and sheet of paper for each of you.

Song

"Reverently and Meekly Now" (*Hymns*, no. 185)

Lesson

For the first portion of this lesson, try to say as little as possible. After singing the hymn, watch the video *Lifting Burdens*. Without speaking, set the timer for five or ten minutes. Read Luke 22:40–46 individually and write down your thoughts, impressions from the Spirit, and any experiences that come to mind. When the time is up, share with your spouse your testimony of the Atonement, along with any thoughts or experiences you feel inspired to share.

Additional Resources

David A Bednar, "Bear Up Their Burdens with Ease," General Conference, Oct. 2014 (lds.org/general-conference/2014/04/bear-up-their-burdens-with-ease).

The Sacrament

Preparation

Gather paper and pencils.

Song

"As Now We Take the Sacrament" (*Hymns*, no. 169)

Lesson

Talk about what you can do together to make the ordinance of the sacrament more meaningful. You may want to read, listen to, or watch one or both of the following talks:

- Cheryl A. Esplin, "The Sacrament—a Renewal for the Soul," General Conference, Oct. 2014 (lds.org/general-conference/2014/10/the-sacrament-a-renewal-for-the-soul).
- Dallin H. Oaks, "Sacrament Meeting and the Sacrament," General Conference, Oct. 2008 (lds.org/general-conference/2008/10/sacrament-meeting-and-the-sacrament).

The sacrament can be a time of renewing our commitments and reviewing our goals and progress. Write down some of your long-term and short-term goals, both spiritual and temporal. Pick goals to reach together as spouses, as well as individually. Seek the guidance of the Lord to select the best goals. Pray for help as you work toward your goals and support your spouse in his or hers. Next week during the sacrament, think about your spiritual goals and how you've done with them. Repent of your mistakes. As you renew your covenants, the Spirit will be with you, and your ability to reach your goals will increase.

Two on the Road to Emmaus

Preparation

Access the Bible video *Christ Appears on the Road to Emmaus* on lds.org (lds.org/bible-videos/videos/christ-appears-on-the-road-to-emmaus).

Song

"Abide with Me" (*Hymns,* no. 166)

Lesson

Consider times when you faced challenges or went through a trial. Share a few of these experiences with each other.

Watch the video *Christ Appears on the Road to Emmaus*, or if you don't have access to the video, read Luke 24:13–33 together.

The two men walking along the road were troubled by what they saw as inconsistencies. Wasn't Christ supposed to save them? He had died, but now others were saying His body was gone. What did all this mean? How might these two men have felt? In your trials, do you ever feel like "darkness deepens" and "help and comforts flee"? Can you see how the Savior was with you, even if you didn't know it at the time? Did having His help change your perspective?

Read Isaiah 4:5. This verse refers to the children of Israel when the Lord led them out of Egypt. As they traveled in the wilderness, He provided a pillar of fire at night, and a cloud of smoke as a covering from the heat in the daytime. Even though the Israelites still had many trials, how might the presence of the fire and cloud have been comforting?

What can you do to invite the Savior into your home and marriage? Some things to consider might be personal and family scripture study, prayer, church attendance, and weekly family home evenings. How is His glory a defense, while the world's "glories pass away"? Commit to doing all you can to make Jesus Christ a part of your marriage so that His glory will be your defense in every trial.

Additional Resources

Henry B. Eyring, "Come Unto Me," General Conference, Apr. 2013 (lds.org/general-conference/2013/04/come-unto-me).

Where Can I Turn for Peace?

Preparation

Find out what time the sun sets and choose a place where you can watch it. Plan your family night activity so it begins just before sunset. You may want to bring a blanket and a treat to share.

Song

Where Can I Turn for Peace?" (*Hymns*, no. 129)

Lesson

If your spot for watching the sunset is a public place, you may be more comfortable having your prayer and song at home. Then head to your predetermined spot to watch the sunset. Bring your scriptures.

Read John 14:16–27. How do we access the peace spoken of in these verses? Consider how the gift of the Holy Ghost fulfills the Savior's promise (see Acts 2:1–4). Watch the sunset. You may want to discuss one or more of the following questions:

- How does the Savior's promise to comfort you help you through your trials?
- During which experiences did you feel the comfort of the Holy Ghost?
- How does the peace the Savior offers differ from the peace the world seeks?

- How can you have that peace in your life even while those around you are in commotion?

Additional Resources

Richard G. Scott, "Make the Exercise of Your Faith Your First Priority," General Conference, Oct. 2014 (lds.org/general-conference/2014/10/make-the-exercise-of-faith-your-first-priority).

Quentin L. Cook, "Personal Peace: The Reward of Righteousness," General Conference, Apr. 2013 (lds.org/general-conference/2013/04/personal-peace-the-reward-of-righteousness).

Becoming Like Him

Becoming

Preparation

Get a puzzle with at least one hundred pieces. If you don't have a puzzle on hand, you might borrow one from a neighbor or relative, or buy one at a dollar store.

Song

"I'm Trying to Be Like Jesus" (*Children's Songbook,* 78)

Lesson

Open your puzzle. Imagine having to put the entire thing together all at once—no testing pieces to see if they fit, no sorting or placing pieces one at time. Now imagine putting the puzzle together in the dark. How long would it take for you to get discouraged and give up?

Jesus taught us in Matthew 5:48, "Be ye therefore perfect, even as your Father which is in heaven is perfect." Do we sometimes try to reach this goal all at once? How long would it take us to give up if we couldn't make mistakes at all? Thankfully, the Lord has provided the Savior and the Atonement to help us overcome our mistakes. Read 2 Nephi 28:30. How is putting a puzzle together like our journey toward perfection? Read the promise in Moroni 10:32. How is putting a puzzle together in the dark similar to trying to become perfect without Jesus Christ?

Do we ever demand perfection of others? Of our marriages? How can we use the principles of the Atonement, forgiveness, and moving forward line upon line to better our relationships and marriage?

Have fun putting your puzzle together. You may want to turn on a general conference talk, audio book, or music while you work on the puzzle.

Additional Resources

Ulisses Soares, "Be Meek and Lowly of Heart," General Conference, Oct. 2013 (lds.org/general-conference/2013/10/be-meek-and-lowly-of-heart).

Gratitude

Preparation

You will need a bulletin board, whiteboard, large poster, or several sturdy papers taped together. You will also need a way to hang the board, poster, or papers.

Song

"Count Your Blessings," (*Hymns*, no. 241)

Lesson

Brainstorm different people from the scriptures or Church history who have been sent on journeys by the Lord. What were some of their challenges? Do you worry about some of the same things these people did?

In the story of Lehi and his family, we learn that almost everyone in the group complained or murmured at some point: Lehi (1 Nephi 16:20), Sariah (1 Nephi 5:1–3), the sons of Ishmael, and of course, Laman and Lemuel. Just like them, we all have moments in our lives when we have trials and want to complain or murmur.

Read 1 Nephi 2:12 and 18:3. What is the difference between Nephi and his brothers?

Read 1 Nephi 16:23 and 18:15–16. In the first example, Nephi acts. He makes a bow and then asks his father where he should hunt for food for the family. How might we act when we are faced with trials? Nephi doesn't do something random; he makes a plan and then asks for further guidance from the Lord through his father, the family patriarch. How do acting with purpose and following divine guidance help us to avoid complaining and be grateful?

In the second example, Nephi can't do anything, yet he praises the Lord. Sometimes our trials are like that too—we can do nothing about them. How does having a greater understanding of God and His plan allow us to look beyond the immediate situation, no matter how grim? What things has He given you that can't be taken away? What does He promise you that you can always be thankful for?

On your poster, write things the Lord has given you forever, and blessings He has promised you if you are faithful. Write down the little things you are grateful for that allow you to act, even when life is hard. Think of experiences you have had, people you have met, and love you have felt. Hang your gratitude poster up where you can see it and add to it.

Additional Resources

Dieter F. Uchtdorf, "Grateful in Any Circumstances," General Conference, Apr. 2014 (lds.org/general-conference/2014/04/grateful-in-any-circumstances).

Dieter F. Uchtdorf, "Your Wonderful Journey Home," General Conference, Apr. 2013 (lds.org/general-conference/2013/04/your-wonderful-journey-home).

Agency

Preparation

Gather items to create an obstacle course. Some ideas might be blankets, boxes, baskets, rope, room dividers, and chairs and other sturdy furniture. Find something to use as a blindfold.

Song

"Choose the Right" (*Hymns*, no. 239)

Lesson

Make an obstacle course around your house or outdoors. Take turns being blindfolded and trying to navigate the course. Try doing the course on your own, and also with the aid of your spouse. How do you feel doing the course while blindfolded? How does having a guide help? How does the course compare to life?

Read Moses 7:32–33, where the Lord responds to Enoch's question of how God can weep. Although Heavenly Father is saddened when we make the wrong choices, He still allows us our agency. We must choose to obey and choose to follow our Savior.

Re-read Moses 7:33. How does this verse apply to marriage? Discuss the following quote by Elder Lynn G. Robbins: "Scripturally, the Lord is very clear with us on this doctrine—you can't 'fall out of love,' because love is something you decide. Agency plays a fundamental role in our relationships with one another. This being true, we must make the conscious decision that we will love our spouse and family with all our heart, soul, and mind; that we will build, not 'fall into,' strong, loving marriages and families."[3]

How can you choose to love each other? How will that choice help you to navigate the challenges and trials you will face in the future?

Additional Resources

L. Tom Perry, "Obedience Through Our Faithfulness," General Conference, Apr. 2014 (lds.org/general-conference/2014/04/obedience-through-our-faithfulness).

---

3. Lynn G. Robbins, "Agency and Love in Marriage," *Ensign,* Oct. 2000 (lds.org/ensign/2000/10/agency-and-love-in-marriage).

Prayer

Preparation

Collect paint, paintbrushes, permanent markers, or other crafting items you can use to decorate a rock.

Song

"Did You Think to Pray?" (*Hymns*, no. 140)

Lesson

Find a rock and wash any dirt off it. While the rock dries, search for a scripture that can be a theme for your family's attitude about prayer. Write the scripture on your rock. If your scripture is too long for your rock, pick a phrase that will fit. For example, if you picked 2 Nephi 32:9, you might choose "Pray always." Decorate your prayer rock together. Make a goal to help each other memorize the scripture. You might try to recite it from memory at your next family night.

We learn from the scriptures that Jesus Christ prayed to the Father in all situations and times (see Matthew 6:9; Matthew 26:36, 39, 42; Mark 1:35; Mark 6:46; John 14:16; John 17; 3 Nephi 17:15). The Savior was constantly turning to God and seeking His Father's will. Christ's example teaches us the importance of prayer. He wants us to reach out to our Heavenly Father and come to know Him as our Savior does.

Read this quote from President James E. Faust: "No earthly authority can separate us from direct access to our Creator. There can never be a mechanical or electronic failure when we pray. There is no limit on the number of times or how long we can pray each day. There is no quota of how many needs we wish to pray for in each prayer. We do not need to go through secretaries or make an appointment to reach the throne of grace. He is reachable at any time or any place."[4]

Put your rock in a place where it will remind you to have morning and evening prayers and to always keep a prayer in your heart. Typically a prayer rock would be placed near your pillow to remind you to pray before you get in bed. Then the rock is set on the floor by the bed so that when you get up, you remember to kneel for morning prayers. You can also find another place, like near the front door, or even on your bathroom countertop where you will see it as you get ready.

---

4. James E. Faust, "The Lifeline of Prayer," General Conference, Apr. 2002 (lds.org/general-conference/2002/04/the-lifeline-of-prayer).

Scriptures

Preparation

Make a copy of the scripture-chase questions on the following page. Get a Book of Mormon you can give away. You can buy one at store.lds.org, at a Church distribution center, or at a used bookstore or a secondhand store. Or use one of your own copies that is in good condition.

Song

"The Iron Rod" (*Hymns*, no. 274)

Lesson

Using your copies of the questions on the following page, have a scripture chase to find the answers in the Book of Mormon. List the chapter and verse next to each question. The person to finish first gets to pick what you have for dessert.

Once you finish, take the Book of Mormon you are giving away and highlight a few of the scriptures you found. Write your testimonies in the front of the book. Either tonight or in the coming days, give your Book of Mormon to someone. Pray for help to know whom to give it to, and the Lord will guide you.

Scripture-Chase Questions

Copy this page and cut on the dotted lines.

- -

Who are we?

Why are we here?

How do we return to our Father in Heaven?

Where can we find comfort in times of sadness or trial?

Who is Jesus Christ?

What is Jesus Christ's role?

How do we know what is right and wrong?

Why are we given commandments?

What is the purpose of prophets?

How can we be missionaries?

- -

Who are we?

Why are we here?

How do we return to our Father in Heaven?

Where can we find comfort in times of sadness or trial?

Who is Jesus Christ?

What is Jesus Christ's role?

How do we know what is right and wrong?

Why are we given commandments?

What is the purpose of prophets?

How can we be missionaries?

- -

Knowledge

Preparation

Find your library card. If you don't have one, get on your local library's website and find out what you need to do to get a card.

Song

"Press Forward Saints" (*Hymns,* no. 81)

Lesson

Read Luke 2:52 and Doctrine and Covenants 88:118 and 93:53. Take a trip to your local library and check out some books. Make sure you check out at least one nonfiction book. You can read it together if you'd like. It might be fun to talk about the things you are learning together.

Additional Resources

"Education," The Church of Jesus Christ of Latter-day Saints (lds. org/topics/education).

Temperance

Preparation

Find a calendar big enough to write menu details on, or copy and enlarge the one-week menu calendar on page 50.

Song

"Do What Is Right" (*Hymns*, no. 237)

Lesson

Temperance is restraint and balance that are developed through self-control. Temperance is about moderation in the things we do, and about mastering our bodies. Think of ways the Savior showed temperance in His life (for example, read Matthew 4, where He was tempted by Satan). We need temperance to help in the Lord's work (see Doctrine and Covenants 12:8). Why would the Lord want us to develop the attribute of temperance?

Read 1 Corinthians 9:24–27. How does being temperate help win a race? In what other ways can temperance be used in our lives? Read the Word of Wisdom in Doctrine and Covenants 89. In what ways could you be more temperate in caring for your bodies?

Talk about the meals you typically eat. What foods do you eat? Are your meals well-balanced? Do you eat food in moderation? One way to apply temperance to your food intake is to plan ahead.

It will help you shop smarter, eat healthier, and reduce meal-time stress.

Create a list of meals you like. You can round them out by adding fruits and vegetables, and by exploring ideas for healthier or meatless meals. Once you have your list, you can transfer your ideas into a meal calendar you can rotate through. It's sometimes fun to leave a few days open to rotate in new foods or seasonal meals. You can build multiple calendars as you experiment with new foods and rotate the calendars for more variety.

Additional Resources

For more ideas on healthy eating, visit the website for the President's Council on Sports, Fitness, and Nutrition fitness.gov/eat-healthy/how-to-eat-healthy/).

Kent D. Watson, "Being Temperate in All Things," General Conference, Oct. 2009 (lds.org/general-conference/2009/10/being-temperate-in-all-things).

"Chapter 42: Let us Conquer Ourselves," *Teachings of the Presidents of the Church: Joseph F. Smith,* 2011, 370–79.

Enlarge and copy this chart.

Meal Plan for Week of _____

Monday	Tuesday	Wednesday	Thursday
Breakfast	Breakfast	Breakfast	Breakfast
Lunch	Lunch	Lunch	Lunch
Dinner	Dinner	Dinner	Dinner

Friday	Saturday	Sunday	Shopping List
Breakfast	Breakfast	Breakfast	
Lunch	Lunch	Lunch	
Dinner	Dinner	Dinner	

Diligence

Preparation

Find a timer to aid in your fitness assessment.

Song

"How Gentle God's Commands" (*Hymns*, no. 125)

Lesson

Did you ever set a goal to become more physically fit? What made the difference between reaching or not reaching that goal?

Heavenly Father has given us many commandments. What do Doctrine and Covenants 130:18–21 and 103:36 teach us about being diligent and keeping the commandments? How can we avoid giving up on obedience like we might give up on a goal to become physically fit? Read Moroni 8:26. How can the Atonement of Jesus Christ provide both relief from our mistakes and power to reach farther than we thought we could? Diligence doesn't imply that we never make a mistake, only that we keep steadily moving forward. Read Mosiah 4:27.

It is important to keep a balance in life. As we avoid focusing too much on one thing, we are happier, make healthier choices, and are better servants of the Lord. One of the greatest gifts our Father in Heaven has given us is our bodies. He wants us to care for them and will help us as we strive for both physical and spiritual health. Do you have a regular exercise program? Can you apply the principle of diligence to establish exercise goals, or to reach those you have already set?

Using the chart on the next page, take turns assessing your fitness levels. Instructions for each test can be found online along with what the healthy standard is for each of you based on your age and gender. Simply do a search for each fitness test by name. Here are some websites that may be helpful to you:

- health.gov/paguidelines/guidelines/chapter4.aspx
- sparkpeople.com/resource/fitness_articles.asp?id=1112
- topendsports.com/testing/hometest.htm
- skinnyms.com/yourathomefitnessassessment/

Fill out the chart and make an attainable goal for the next six weeks.

Consider exercising together as a couple or joining a fitness class or a city sports team. Find a way to support one another with a focus on individual needs and achievement. No matter where you are right now, diligently move forward, and don't give up when you make a mistake. Be sure to celebrate along the way.

Additional Resources

Jorg Klebingat, "Approaching the Throne of God with Confidence," General Conference, Oct. 2014 (lds.org/general-conference/2014/10/approaching-the-throne-of-god-with-confidence).

Make two copies of this chart.

Fitness Assessment and Goals for _____

Test	Test Results	Healthy Standard	Six-Week Goal
Pushups (upper-body strength)			
Sit-ups or crunches (core strength)			
Squats or step-ups (lower-body strength)			
Sit and reach (flexibility)			
Mile walk or run (aerobic)			

Covenants

Preparation

You will need to go to a temple, or display a picture of one.

Song

"Families Can Be Together Forever" (*Hymns*, no. 300)

Lesson

Go where you can see the temple. Keep in mind the temple grounds are closed on Monday evenings. You will still be able to walk around the temple or park somewhere close. If you are not close to a temple, look at a picture of one.

Read Hebrews 4:16 and Doctrine and Covenants 110 together.

Temple covenants are vital to our eternal progression and salvation. They give us power. They allow us to access our Savior's Atonement more fully and come to know Him more deeply. If kept, our covenants allow us to "boldly approach the throne of God" (Hebrews 4:16), knowing we are worthy to ask for His mercy and help. The Lord wants to bless us in His house, but we must make the commitment to be there. Take a walk around the temple. As you walk consider one or more of these questions together:

- What do we need to do to go to the temple and make covenants if we haven't already done so?

- How can we make our temple experiences more spiritual?
- Can we set aside a time for regular temple attendance?
- Do we have a picture of the temple displayed in our house?

Additional Resources

"Preparing to Enter the Holy Temple," lds.org (lds.org/manual/preparing-to-enter-the-holy-temple/preparing-to-enter-the-holy-temple).

Thomas S. M0onson, "The Holy Temple—A Beacon to the World," General Conference, Apr. 2011 (lds.org/general-conference/2011/04/the-holy-temple-a-beacon-to-the-world).

Gaye Strathearn, "Let Us Therefore Come Boldly to the Throne of Grace," BYU Women's Conference, May 1, 2014 (ce.byu.edu/cw/womensconference/pdf/archive/2014/gaye_strathearn.pdf).

Service

Preparation

For this lesson you will do a service project, so you'll need to decide on one and prepare for it. If necessary, plan the project during family home evening and carry it out another night. See the lesson for ideas.

Song

"Because I Have Been Given Much" (*Hymns*, no. 219)

Lesson

Read Mosiah 2:17, then do your service project. Here are some ideas:

- Help someone with yard work or housework.
- Ask your bishop or Relief Society president if they are working on humanitarian kits or service projects you can help with.
- Look online for local children's homes or charities for a list of supplies they need. Donate items you have on hand, or make a trip to buy specific items.
- Put together and deliver a bag of food to a homeless shelter or food bank.
- Volunteer at a soup kitchen.
- Make dinner for a neighbor.

- Volunteer to watch a family member's, friend's, or ward member's children while they go on a date or have time to themselves.
- If you know how to sew, work with wood, crochet, or build something, work on a project together that you can give away.
- Help someone who is moving.
- Visit an elderly or sick person.

Hope

Preparation

Gather paper, pencils, and envelopes.

Song

"I Know that My Redeemer Lives" (*Hymns*, no. 136)

Lesson

Moroni, the son of Mormon, was born in a time of great wickedness. He lived to see the death of all his people. Of this experience, Moroni writes in Mormon 8:5, "My father hath been slain in battle, and all my kinsfolk, and I have not friends nor whither to go; and how long the Lord will suffer that I may live I know not."

Later we learn that Mormon sent letters to Moroni describing things that were happening, and also giving him advice and counsel. Read Moroni 9:25. In the midst of all this sorrow, what did Moroni have to be hopeful about?

How can Christ be your hope? Read Mosiah 16:9. In what ways does our Savior offer a hope that cannot fail?

Read and discuss this quote by President Gordon B. Hinckley:

One thing we do know. Like the Polar Star in the heavens, regardless of what the future holds, there stands the Redeemer of the world, the Son of God, certain and sure as the anchor of our immortal lives. He is the rock of our salvation, our strength, our comfort, the very focus of our faith.

In sunshine and in shadow we look to Him, and He is there to assure and smile upon us.[5]

Think about your future. What do you want? Where do you want to be? Write letters to each other to be opened in five or ten years. Write about your dreams and goals, but also include down your testimony of Jesus Christ. Express your love to your spouse. Seal your letters and put them somewhere safe. When the time comes to open the letters, you can read them and then write new letters. Reseal all the letters and save them for another five to ten years.

Additional Resources

Joseph B. Wirthlin, "The Abundant Life," General Conference, Apr. 2006 (lds.org/general-conference/2006/04/the-abundant-life).

---

5. Gordon B. Hinckley, "We Look to Christ," General Conference, Apr. 2002 (lds.org/general-conference/2002/04/we-look-to-christ).

Faith

Preparation

Arrange to visit a Church historical site or visitor's center near you. Most are open on Monday evenings, but check the hours before you go. If there are no local historical sites or visitor's centers, choose one of the alternate activities listed in the lesson.

Song

"Come, Come Ye Saints" (*Hymns*, no. 30)

Lesson

There are many stories from Church history about how early Latter-Day Saints demonstrated their faith in Jesus Christ. Read JST James 2:15. How did the pioneers show their faith by their actions? Go to a local visitor's center or Church history site and look for examples of early members' faith in the Savior. Share those examples with each other.

If the visitor's centers and Church history sites are too far away, here are some alternate activity ideas:

- Find information about the first Latter-day Saints who lived in your area. If possible, take a drive or walk to see the site of their homes, or the cemetery where they are buried.

- Visit important places from your life or the lives of your family. Recount experiences of faith that are connected to those places.
- Retell stories from the lives of your ancestors that illustrate their faith in Jesus Christ. Or tell a story of how your faith helped you.
- Make a picture book of your favorite faith story to share with your future children or nieces and nephews.

Additional Resources

A list of Church history sites and visitor's centers, along with contact information, is found at lds.org/locations/visitors-centers.

Charity

Preparation

Access the story "Toothpaste on the Mirror" by Bryce R. Peterson in the September 2008 *Ensign* (lds.org/ensign/2008/09/toothpaste-on-the-mirror).

Song

"Love At Home" (*Hymns*, no. 294)

Lesson

Even with our best intentions, marriage will sometimes be hard. It might feel like everything is going wrong or that our relationship is falling apart. Learning to live with and support each other requires daily care and the best kind of love. Read Moroni 7:45–48. How does someone with charity treat his or her spouse? If "charity never faileth," what hope does that give to a marriage built on charity?

Read or listen to the story "Toothpaste on the Mirror." A good way to strengthen a marriage is to focus on your spouse's positive traits. There will always be things you would like to change, but dwelling on them can overshadow your spouse's good traits and skew your perspective.

Play the Good Things game. The husband starts by saying something good about his wife that starts with the letter "A." The wife goes next, saying something she likes about her husband that starts with the letter "B." Continue through the alphabet, taking turns listing good qualities with each letter. If you want, start over and do it again, with the wife going first. Make it a challenge by listing things that haven't already been said.

Additional Resources

Russell M. Nelsen, "Nurturing Marriage," General Conference, Apr. 2006 (lds.org/general-conference/2006/04/nurturing-marriage).

Humility

Preparation

Access the video *Our Hands, His Hands; Our Hearts, His Heart* in the media library on lds.org (lds.org/media-library/video/2011-04-005-our-hands-his-hands-our-hearts-his-heart). Get out a card game or board game. If you want more players for your game, invite another couple over for this lesson.

Song

"Be Thou Humble" (*Hymns,* no. 130)

Lesson

True humility is a realization of how much we need our Savior, a recognition that without Him, we can do nothing, but that with Him we can do everything. Read Ether 12:27. How can our weakness help us come to know Jesus Christ better? Read 2 Corinthians 12:7–10. Have you or someone you know prayed for relief from sickness or weakness? How can the trials we face, even those with no end in sight, humble us and bring us to the Savior?

Watch the video *Our Hands, His Hands; Our Hearts, His Heart.* What blessings have you seen because you humbled yourself or because someone else was humble enough to ask for help? How can both allowing your spouse to help you and helping your spouse be a reflection of our dependence on and relationship with the Savior? In what other ways can humility strengthen your marriage?

Play your board game or card game. Try to keep a spirit of humility by showing good sportsmanship.

Additional Resources

Gerald Caussé, "For When I Am Weak, Then I Am Strong," BYU Devotional Address, Dec. 3, 2013 (speeches.byu.edu/?act =viewitem&id=2157).

Virtue

Preparation

Gather any supplies you might need to help you with your memorization. See the lesson for more details.

Song

"Dearest Children, God Is Near You" (*Hymns*, no. 96)

Lesson

In *Preach My Gospel,* we read: "Virtue is a pattern of thought and behavior based on high moral standards. It includes chastity and purity."[6] In what ways should virtue be a part of your marriage? Consider things like pornography, TV shows or movies you watch, games you play, online relationships, balancing relationships with friends, and how you can always communicate openly, honestly, and trustingly with each other.

The Savior wants us to become as He is. He wants us to return, pure and confident, to our Father in Heaven. Read Doctrine and Covenants 121:45 and Philippians 4:8. How can virtuous thoughts help us stay morally clean? How can you get rid of bad thoughts or images that sneak into your mind?

---

6. *Preach My Gospel: A Guide to Missionary Service* (Salt Lake City, UT: The Church of Jesus Christ of Latter-day Saints, 2004), 118.

Memorize a hymn, scripture, or quote together to turn to when you want to clear your mind of bad thoughts (for example, Doctrine and Covenants 121:45 or Philippians 4:8). To help you memorize, you may want to try some of the following:

- Learn one small phrase at a time.
- Go back and forth, each of you taking a turn saying one word at a time.
- Put the words to music.
- Write it down and erase a few words at a time as you memorize them.
- Write down each word on a strip of paper and mix it up before challenging your spouse to put it in the right order again.

Additional Resources

Elaine S. Dalton, "A Return to Virtue," General Conference, Oct. 2008 (lds.org/general-conference/2008/10/a-return-to-virtue).

Here are two talks about how memorizing hymns and scriptures can bless your lives:

Boyd K. Packer, "Inspiring Music—Worthy Thoughts," General Conference, Apr. 1973 (lds.org/general-conference/1973/10/inspiring-music-worthy-thoughts).

Richard G. Scott, "He Lives," General Conference, Oct. 1999 (lds.org/general-conference/1999/10/he-lives).

Light

Preparation

Choose whether you want to do dinner or dessert as a part of this lesson. Prepare the necessary food, and set up a romantic table with candles for light.

Song

"Brightly Beams Our Father's Mercy" (*Hymns,* no. 335)

Lesson

Using the opening song for reference, discuss how our examples should be a light that leads people to Jesus Christ. Read Doctrine and Covenants 50:24 and 88:42–44. How can you increase the light of Christ within you? How might the Lord have placed you in someone's path so you can give light to each other?

Enjoy your dinner or dessert by the light of candles.

Additional Resources

Boyd K. Packer, "The Atonement," General Conference, Oct. 2012 (lds.org/general-conference/2012/10/the-atonement).

Gerald Caussé, "Ye Are No More Strangers," General Conference, Oct. 2013 (lds.org/general-conference/2013/10/ye-are-no-more-strangers).

Prove Me

Preparation

Arrange to visit a place where you can view God's creations (see the lesson for ideas).

Song

"How Firm a Foundation" (*Hymns,* no. 85). If you have time, sing all the verses.

Lesson

While we are on earth to learn and grow, we can trust that we do not have to go it alone. As we come to know our Father in Heaven and Savior better, we learn that we can prove Them. We prove Them as constant, unchanging, and loving. They will always keep Their promises when we keep ours.

Read Abraham 3:25–27 and Malachi 3:10. How does the Lord prove us? What has He sent us here to do? In the example of tithing, how does the Lord ask us to prove Him? How can we prove Him by doing the things He asks of us?

Read Doctrine and Covenants 84:82 and Luke 12:6–7. The Lord knows and loves all His creations. We can rely on Him to care for us. As we prove to Him and to ourselves that we are capable of becoming who He wants us to be, He will be with us each step of the way.

Go to a place where you can see God's creations. Here are some suggestions:

- Visit a zoo, an aquarium, or an aviary.
- Go to a farm.
- Visit a garden or park.
- Take a hike or walk.
- Go horseback riding.
- Visit the Humane Society.

Additional Resources

Patricia T. Holland, "Fear Not," BYU Devotional Address, Sept. 15, 1987 (speeches.byu.edu/?act=viewitem&id=1282).

Marcos A. Aidukaitis, "If Ye Lack Wisdom," General Conference, Oct. 2014 (lds.org/general-conference/2014/04/if-ye-lack-wisdom).

His Work and His Glory

Pre-Earth Life

Preparation

Get the equipment you will need to play a sport of your choice, or get tickets to a sporting event. You may want to invite other couples to join you for this family night or even just for the activity.

Song

"I Lived in Heaven" (*Children's Songbook*, 4)

Lesson

How do athletes prepare for a sporting event? What is the value of a coach? In team sports, what is the value of the other members of the team?

Like athletes preparing for the big game, we learned and prepared in our pre-earth life. Read Abraham 3:22–28. Who in your lives might be compared to a coach that teaches the plan of our Father in Heaven and helps you remember your training? Who around you might be compared to team members? Are there spectators that cheer you on or discourage you? Even though we don't remember all the training we received before we came to earth, we have been prepared for this journey. Read Doctrine and Covenants 138:56. How does knowing you were prepared help you face mortality and make good decisions now?

Play your favorite sport or go to a sporting event. Some ideas are basketball, tennis, baseball, volleyball, Frisbee, or soccer.

Additional Resources

Henry B. Eyring, "Daughters in the Covenant," General Conference, Apr. 2014 (lds.org/general-conference/2014/04/daughters-in-the-covenant).

Gary E. Stevenson, "Your Four Minutes," General Conference, Apr. 2014 (lds.org/general-conference/2014/04/your-four-minutes).

Earth as a Witness

Preparation

For this lesson you will need a camera, one for each of you if possible. If not, drawing paper and pencils can be substituted.

Song

"God Is Love" (*Hymns,* no. 87)

Lesson

Each of you share something beautiful from nature that you observed today. If you didn't notice anything, when was the last time you did? In the scriptures we learn that Jesus Christ created the earth under the direction of God the Father. Read Moses 2 and consider the love that went into the Creation. What does observing the world around you teach you about Christ? How can you take more time to notice all the beautiful things in nature?

Get your cameras and go for a nature walk. Anywhere will do, even if it's just the sidewalk outside your home. As you walk, take photos that might represent different aspects of the Creation: animals, plants, water, earth, the heavens, darkness, and light. At the end of your walk, take a photo of your spouse. He or she was created by Heavenly Father and Jesus Christ. If you don't have a camera, draw some of the things you see. Simple drawings are fine;

you don't need to be an artist to recognize the beauty of God's creations.

When you get home, share your photos with each other. Can you see God's love in the images? Read Alma 30:41, 44. How can nature bring you closer to the Savior? Put your photos where you will be reminded to look for God's love in the world around you. You could print them and hang them in your home, post them on a social media site, or use them as wallpaper on your phone, tablet, or computer.

One Flesh

Preparation

Arrange to re-create the first date you went on together, or another date that has special meaning to both of you.

Song

"Love One Another" (*Hymns*, no. 308)

Lesson

Read Mark 10:6–8. These are some of the Savior's words about marriage. Go on your re-created date. If you have time before, during, or after your date, think about or discuss how your lives have changed since your first date and how you've become "one flesh." How does loving your spouse like the Savior loves you bring you closer?

Additional Resources

Henry B. Eyring, "To My Grandchildren," General Conference, Oct. 2013 (lds.org/general-conference/2013/10/to-my-grandchildren).

Matthew O. Richardson, "Three Principles of Marriage," *Ensign,* Apr. 2005 (lds.org/ensign/2005/04/three-principles-of-marriage).

Revelation

Preparation

If you've received your patriarchal blessing, bring it to family night.

Song

"Let the Holy Spirit Guide" (*Hymns*, no. 143)

Lesson

Read Doctrine and Covenants 8:1–3 and 9:7–9. What are some of the ways Jesus Christ speaks to us today? How can we know what He and our Father in Heaven want us to do?

One source of revelation is a patriarchal blessing. Share yours with each other. If you haven't received your patriarchal blessing, talk to your bishop so he can help you start the process.

Additional Resources

Richard G. Scott, "Agency and Answers: Recognizing Revelation," *Ensign,* July 2014 (lds.org/ensign/2014/06/agency-and-answers-recognizing-revelation).

Henry B. Eyring, "Continuing Revelation," General Conference, Oct. 2014 (lds.org/general-conference/2014/10/continuing-revelation).

Carlos A. Godoy, "The Lord Has a Plan for Us," General Conference, Oct. 2014 (lds.org/general-conference/2014/10/the-lord-has-a-plan-for-us).

Cease to Be Idle

Preparation

Get out your cleaning supplies.

Song

"Put Your Shoulder to the Wheel" (*Hymns*, no. 252)

Lesson

Read Genesis 3:19 and Doctrine and Covenants 88:124. How does the Lord feel about work? Read John 9:3–4. What can we learn from the Savior's example? What work has the Lord sent you here to do?

Have a cleaning scavenger hunt. Copy the cleaning idea list on the next page, and cut out the chores that apply to your home. Put them in a hat or basket. Each of you draw five (or more if you're feeling ambitious). Have a race to see who finishes cleaning first. Make sure you do a good job! You might want to listen to music while you work.

Additional Resources

H. David Burton, "The Blessing of Work," *Liahona,* Dec. 2009 (lds. org/liahona/2009/12/the-blessing-of-work).

Cleaning Scavenger Hunt

Copy this list and cut into strips.

Wash all the surfaces in one room.

Dust one room.

Wash one window, inside and out.

Sweep a floor.

Vacuum a floor.

Pick up and put away ten items.

Load or unload the dishwasher, or wash the dishes by hand.

Take out the trash.

Mop a floor.

Organize your junk drawer or mail pile.

Clean a mirror.

Make a bed.

Fold a load of laundry.

Start a load of laundry.

Clean the bathtub or shower.

Clean a sink.

Clean a toilet.

Prophets

Preparation

If you decide to do the recording activity, you will need a way to record your voice.

Song

"Joseph Smith's First Prayer" (*Hymns*, no. 26)

Lesson

How does Jesus Christ direct His Church today? Read Doctrine and Covenants 1:38 and Amos 3:7. Have you ever had an experience when you knew a prophet or Apostle was truly called of God?

Do one of the following activities:

- Find a favorite quote from a prophet and post a link along with your testimonies of modern prophets to a social media site.
- Follow the advice of Elder Neil L. Anderson to record yourselves reading the story of the First Vision, found in Joseph Smith—History 1.[7] It might be fun to take turns reading portions. You can listen to it in your car, while doing chores, or even while getting ready in the morning.

---

7. Neil L. Anderson, "Joseph Smith," General Conference, Oct. 2014 (lds.org/generalconference/2014/10/joseph-smith).

- If you haven't done so, memorize the order and names of the latter-day prophets or the twelve Apostles. Quiz each other.
- Pick one prophet or Apostle to learn more about. Read stories of their lives and their testimonies.

Additional Resources

Russell M. Nelson, "Sustaining the Prophets," General Conference, Oct. 2014 (lds.org/general-conference/2014/10/sustaining-the-prophets).

Carol F. McConkie, "Live According to the Words of the Prophets," General Conference, Oct. 2014 (lds.org/general-conference/2014/10/live-according-to-the-words-of-the-prophets).

General Conference

Preparation

Watch general conference and take notes as you are inspired with thoughts and feelings.

Song

Sing a favorite hymn from general conference. The music is usually listed on lds.org shortly after conference. Just click on the general conference link in the Quick Links section (lds.org/general-conference).

Lesson

Take a few minutes to go over your notes from conference. When you are ready, share your favorite talks, quotes, or thoughts. Read Doctrine and Covenants 1:38. Make a few goals and a plan to follow the counsel given.

Additional Resources

Dieter F. Uchtdorf, "General Conference, No Ordinary Blessing," *Ensign,* Sept. 2013 (lds.org/liahona/2011/09/general-conference-no-ordinary-blessing).

Priesthood and the Family

Preparation

Find a copy of "The Family: A Proclamation to the World" or access it online (lds.org/topics/family-proclamation). Prepare for the activity (see the lesson for details).

Song

"Love Is Spoken Here" (*Children's Songbook*, 190)

Lesson

Read "The Family: A Proclamation to the World." How do our divinely appointed roles allow us to work together as husband and wife in unity and harmony? How can we strengthen each other? Read 1 Corinthians 11:11. Talk about your future family and the children you hope to have. What do you want them to know about Heavenly Father's plan for families and their worth and divinely appointed roles? How can you strengthen your family in the midst of the voices of the world? Pick an aspect from the family proclamation to work on together.

Go on a bike ride or run or walk together. If it's cold outside, go to a fitness center or an indoor track, or go sledding or ice skating.

Additional Resources

Carole M. Stephens, "Do We Know What We Have?" General Conference, Oct. 2013 (lds.org/general-conference/2013/10/do-we-know-what-we-have).

Dallin H. Oaks, "The Keys and Authority of the Priesthood," General Conference, Apr. 2014 (lds.org/general-conference/2014/04/the-keys-and-authority-of-the-priesthood).

Creating

Preparation

Access the video *Create* on lds.org (lds.org/media-library/video/2009-02-06-create). Make arrangements to attend or visit a local museum, play, or musical performance.

Song

"For the Beauty of the Earth" (*Hymns,* 92)

Lesson

Watch the video *Create*. Attend a play or musical performance or visit a museum.

Additional Resources

Dieter F. Uchtdorf, "Happiness, Your Heritage," General Conference, Apr. 2008 (lds.org/general-conference/2008/10/happiness-your-heritage).

Mary Ellen Smoot, "We are Creators," General Conference, Apr. 2000 (lds.org/general-conference/2000/04/we-are-creators).

Zion

Preparation

Gather the supplies for a service project you can do in secret.

Song

"Israel, Israel, God Is Calling" (*Hymns*, no. 7)

Lesson

What are the qualities of a Zion people? (See Moses 7:18; 4 Nephi 1:15–18; Doctrine and Covenants 101:6–7.) How is the Savior's relationship with Heavenly Father an example of how we can build Zion? (See Doctrine and Covenants 50:43; John 5:19, 30.) How can you establish Zion in your home?

Pick a service project to do in secret. Seek the Lord's guidance to know who needs your help, and try to remain anonymous. Here are some ideas:

- Leave a treat or kind note for someone.
- Shovel a neighbor's driveway and walk, or clean snow off their car.
- Rake leaves in someone's yard.
- Pick up trash in your neighborhood.
- Leave food or clothing for someone in need.
- At a restaurant, pay for the meal of a person you don't know.

- Go to a store and tape enough money to buy something to the item with a note saying, "Enjoy this secret act of kindness!"
- Make a "date night" kit for a couple you know with an inexpensive card game or movie and a pack of microwave popcorn. Leave it on their doorstep.
- Create a "survival kit" using items from the dollar store. Give it to a person who is ill, to someone who has a new baby (or to a child with a new sibling), or to anyone who has a big change coming up.

Trials

Preparation

Gather the supplies you will need for an emergency preparedness activity (see the lesson for ideas). Prepare for the activity you choose.

Song

"God Speed the Right" (*Hymns*, no. 106)

Lesson

Read Doctrine and Covenants 121:7–8 and 122:7–9. Why do we have trials? What can we learn from them? How do we endure them well?

Since we have been sent to earth to be tested, we know trials will come. Read the following quote from Thomas S. Monson: "We live in turbulent times. Often the future is unknown; therefore, it behooves us to prepare for uncertainties. When the time for decision arrives, the time for preparation is past."[8]

What can we do now to be spiritually ready for future trials that might come? What can we do to be physically ready?

Spend the rest of your family night going over your emergency preparedness supplies. Emergency preparedness can become

---

8. Thomas S. Monson, "Are We Prepared?" *Ensign,* Sept. 2014 (lds.org/ensign/2014/09/are-we-prepared).

overwhelming. Just as the Lord doesn't expect you to complete your spiritual preparedness all at once, He knows that physically preparing for trials also takes time. What is important is that you are taking consistent steps in that direction. Pick one thing you can work on. Here are some ideas:

- Check your smoke detectors and carbon monoxide detectors.
- Make sure your hot water heater is strapped down.
- Be sure you know where your flashlights, emergency supplies, and important documents are located.
- Create an emergency plan that includes your emergency contacts and a safe meeting place.
- Set aside emergency cash. Make sure it is in small bills.
- Start building a water or food supply. Under beds, tables, and couches might be the only space you have for storage right now, but be creative.
- Put together a 72-hour kits for each of you.
- Check your clothing supplies. Do both of you have winter clothes and good walking shoes?
- Assemble a first-aid kit.
- Make a plan to get out of debt.

For more information, visit the Emergency Preparedness and Response page on lds.org (lds.org/topics/emergency-preparedness).

Additional Resources

Henry B. Eyring, "Mountains to Climb," General Conference, Apr. 2012 (lds.org/general-conference/2012/04/mountains-to-climb).

Quentin L. Cook, "'Hope Ya Know, We Had a Hard Time,'" General Conference, Oct. 2008 (lds.org/general-conference/2008/10/hope-ya-know-we-had-a-hard-time).

Stand Still

Preparation

Find a place to go stargazing. If you live near a planetarium, you may want to check out their show schedule.

Song

"The Lord Is My Shepherd" (*Hymns*, no. 108)

Lesson

Read Exodus 14:10–12. Have you ever reached a point when you just couldn't do anything else to change your situation or achieve a goal? Did you wonder how you got to that place? Read Exodus 14:13. What happens when we turn our worries and struggles over to the Lord and stand still? Read the rest of Exodus 14. How did the Lord protect Israel? How can this story relate to you?

Read Doctrine and Covenants 88:4–10. While our abilities are limited, there is never a limit to the Savior's power. Because of His Atonement, we are never left to face our enemies alone. Sometimes we have to wait. Sometimes the Lord wants us to stand still and trust in His power. What are some ways you can be still in your life?

Go stargazing.

Additional Resources

Jeffrey R. Holland, "An High Priest of Good Things to Come," General Conference, Oct. 1999 (lds.org/general-conference/1999/10/an-high-priest-of-good-things-to-come).

M. Russell Ballard, "Be Still and Know that I Am God," CES Devotional for Young Adults, May 4, 2014 (lds.org/broadcasts/article/ces-devotionals/2014/01/be-still-and-know-that-i-am-god).

Family History: Temple Work

Preparation

Access familysearch.org with your lds.org username and password. If you don't have an account at lds.org, set one up. If you are new to Family Search, you may want to schedule time to go to a family history center or invite someone who is familiar with the process to come to your family night and teach you.

Song

"Families Can Be Together Forever" (*Hymns*, no. 300)

Lesson

We know the Savior spent time in the spirit world before He was resurrected. While there He prepared the way for the gospel to be preached to those who had died without the essential ordinances. Read 1 Peter 3:18–20. In 1918, President Joseph F. Smith had a vision of the spirit world and the Savior's visit there, and also of the work being done among those who are in spirit prison. Read Doctrine and Covenants 138:46–60. What is your role in this work?

There are many ways to help with family history work. Go online to familysearch.org and pull up your family trees. Look through them together. Did you learn anything new about your family? What about your spouse's family? Depending on how much experience you have, here are some things you can do for the remainder of the lesson:

- Post your own photo and memories. Family history starts with you.
- Familiarize yourself with how Family Search works. Learn how to attach sources, find people, and reserve names for the temple. Most of this is easy to figure out, and if you have questions, there are many resources available, including a link on the home page of familysearch.org that will help you find a family history center and people to help you.
- Find names for the temple. If all the works seems to be done for your direct line, use the "Cousins" feature with the "Descendancy" view to show all of a person's descendants, up to four generations at time. A green temple icon indicates that a person has work ready to be done.
- Add memories, photos, documents, and other sources to your family tree. For some of your ancestors, there may be photos you can look at and information you can read.
- Go to the app section on the Family Search homepage. Learn how to use the apps, which are designed to make family history work easier, more accessible, and portable.
- Learn how to index names for the temple. A great video about the power and blessings of indexing is *Redeeming the Dead Redeemed Me* (lds.org/media-library/video/2014-06-01-redeeming-the-dead-redeemed-me).

Additional Resources

Spencer J. Condie, "The Savior's Visit to the Spirit World," *Ensign,* July 2003 (lds.org/ensign/2003/07/the-saviors-visit-to-the-spirit-world).

Allen F. Packer, "The Book," General Conference, Oct. 2014 (lds.org/general-conference/2014/10/the-book).

96

Family History: Stories

Preparation

Arrange for a visit, video call, or phone call with one of your family members. Tell the person you want to interview him or her to ask a few questions for your family history. Explain that you would like to record the conversation. Choose questions from the suggestions below, or come up with your own questions. It is helpful to send the family member a copy of your questions in advance, to give them time to decide what to share. You can also download the Family Search–Memories app on familysearch.org and use it on your smart phone or tablet. It has a recorder and syncs with your online family tree.

Song

"The Hearts of the Children" (*Children's Songbook*, 92)

Lesson

Interview the family member you have chosen. As you talk, record some of his or her stories. Here are a few questions you might want to ask.

- What do you remember about your baptism?
- How did you gain a testimony of Jesus Christ?
- Where did you meet your husband/wife?
- What challenges did you face when you were newlyweds?

- What was growing up like?
- Where have you lived?
- How many siblings do you have?
- What was your favorite vacation?
- What kind of schooling or job did you have?
- What was the most challenging Church calling you've had?
- How many children do you have?
- Do you have special memories from your wedding day or your first time through the temple?
- What was your favorite thing to do with your family?
- What difference have the gospel and the Savior made in your life?

As you chat, take turns asking questions. Listen sincerely and follow up with appropriate questions related to what the person is telling you. You may learn some things you weren't expecting. Find a way to preserve the stories that were shared.

Missionary Work

Song

"I'll Go Where You Want Me to Go" (*Hymns*, no. 270)

Lesson

Read the following scriptures: Acts 9:17–20; Enos 1:4–9; Mosiah 18:8–10; and Mosiah 27:32–37. What happens to people as they come to know Jesus Christ? Remember the story of Ammon and the sons of Mosiah who went to the Lamanites to share the gospel. Read Alma 26:26–31, 37, and discuss the following questions:

- What trials did Ammon and his brethren face in preaching the gospel?
- What fears or concerns do you have about sharing the gospel?
- What gave Ammon and the others faith to keep going, even in the face of failure and discouragement?
- What blessings came to the sons of Mosiah as they shared the gospel?
- What blessings has the Lord promised you? (See Doctrine and Covenants 18:15.)
- What can you and your spouse do to share the gospel?

Make a list of people you know and interact with who are not members of the Church, or have left the Church or become inactive.

Don't worry about whether they seem like people you can share the gospel with or not—just write down their names. Pray for missionary experiences, together and individually. As you pray, keep your list of people in mind. Trust that the Lord will make you equal to any task He prompts you to do. He will prepare the way for you and turn your efforts into miraculous experiences.

Additional Resources

M. Russell Ballard, "Put Your Trust in the Lord," General Conference, Oct. 2013 (lds.org/general-conference/2013/10/put-your-trust-in-the-lord).

David A. Bednar, "Come and See," General Conference, Oct. 2014 (lds.org/general-conference/2014/10/come-and-see).

Come and See

Preparation

Make treats to give to your neighbors, with a card or note introducing yourselves.

Song

"Called to Serve" (*Hymns,* no. 249)

Lesson

How are your missionary efforts going? Take a few minutes to talk about missionary experiences or promptings you've had, and review any missionary goals you've made together. If you haven't made a missionary goal, consider making one.

Read John 1:35–51. What did Jesus and those who followed Him say to others who asked about Him? How does Jesus show that He individually knows those He calls? As we reach out to others and say "Come and see," we invite them to a Savior who knows and loves them perfectly. He will always know the best way to reach them.

Sometimes we need to go out and get to know those around us better. Take your treats and cards and walk around your neighborhood. Get better acquainted with people you live by. Look for opportunities to serve them. As you develop sincere friendships with them, pray for opportunities to invite them to "Come and see."

Additional Resources

"How do I Find people to Teach?" *Preach My Gospel: a Guide to Missionary Service,* 2004, 155–74 (lds.org/manual/preach-my-gospel-a-guide-to-missionary-service/how-do-i-find-people-to-teach).

M. Russell Ballard, "Following Up," General Conference, Apr. 2014 (lds.org/general-conference/2014/04/following-up).

Angels Are Near You

Preparation

Gather some paper, pencils, and envelopes.

Song

"Come unto Jesus" (*Hymns,* no. 117)

Lesson

The Lord has promised that His angels will aid us as we strive to do all we were sent to earth to do. Read Doctrine and Covenants 84:88. Have you felt the presence of angels during certain times in your life? Read Moroni 7:22–31. What is the role of angels?

Elder Jeffrey R. Holland said:

> *I have spoken here of heavenly help, of angels dispatched to bless us in time of need. But when we speak of those who are instruments in the hand of God, we are reminded that not all angels are from the other side of the veil. Some of them we walk with and talk with—here, now, every day. Some of them reside in our own neighborhoods. Some of them gave birth to us, and in my case, one of them consented to marry me. Indeed heaven never seems closer than when we see the love of God manifested in the*

kindness and devotion of people so good and so pure that angelic is the only word that comes to mind.[9]

Think of someone in your life who has brought you closer to Jesus Christ—someone who has been an angel in your time of need. Write a letter to this person to express thanks for his or her help. You may want to bear your testimony. When you finish, deliver the letters.

---

9. Jeffrey R. Holland, "The Ministry of Angels," General Conference, Oct. 2008 (lds.org/general-conference/2008/10/the-ministry-of-angels).

Centered on Him

Valentine's Day

Preparation

Unless you are going with the no-money option, each person will need five dollars.

Song

"My Heavenly Father Loves Me" (*Children's Songbook*, 228).

Lesson

Heavenly Father shows His love to His children in so many ways. Read John 13:34. Jesus wants us to love each other as He loves us.

For Valentine's Day, celebrate the many ways your spouse shows love to you, just as Heavenly Father and Jesus Christ show Their love to us. Love is something we do all the time. With the song "My Heavenly Father Loves Me" as a guide, think of five ways your spouse shows love to you using your five senses. For example:

- Touch: Does he share his favorite warm blanket with you or let you put your ice-cold feet against him to get warm?
- Taste: Does she know your favorite treat, or is there a special food you associate with good experiences with her?
- Hear: Does he say kind things or sing silly songs when you are sad?

- Sight: What about her do you love to see? Her smile? A way she does service? Does she create a beautiful space you enjoy being in with her?
- Smell: What smells remind you of his love?

Copy the following page and cut it in half. Each of you should fill out a questionnaire, stating the ways your spouse shows his or her love for you. Then, visit the nearest dollar store, with five dollars for each spouse to spend. Using your questionnaire as a guide, have a scavenger hunt to find items representing each of the five things you listed (for example, lip balm if you feel your spouse's love when they smile at you, or socks because they let you warm your cold feet on them). When you finish, share your items with each other, or wrap them up with your questionnaire and give them to each other on Valentine's Day.

Alternate (no-money) option: Instead of going to the store, have the scavenger hunt around the house, finding or making things that represent your spouse's love. Wrap them up with the questionnaire explaining why you chose the things you did. If you want to wait for Valentine's Day to give your spouse the items and your spouse might miss something you want to use, take a photo or draw a picture of it instead.

Valentine's Day Questionnaire
Copy this page and cut on the dotted lines.

- -

I know you love me when you . . .

Taste:

Touch:

Sight:

Smell:

Hear:

- -

I know you love me when you . . .

Taste:

Touch:

Sight:

Smell:

Hear:

- -

Easter

Preparation

This lesson is designed to be done in the morning. You may need to adjust your schedule so you can do the lesson on a day other than Monday.

Find out what time the sun rises. Locate a place where you can watch it. You may want to take warm clothing, a blanket, and some hot chocolate.

Song

"I Believe in Christ" (*Hymns*, no. 134)

Lesson

Go to the place where you will watch the sunrise. If you haven't already sung your song and had your opening prayer, do so now. Read the story of Jesus Christ's Resurrection in John 20:1–18. As you watch the sunrise, think about or discuss these questions:

- How does the cycle of the sun setting and rising symbolize the Savior's Resurrection and Atonement?
- How is the sun's light and warmth a symbol of Jesus Christ?
- What has Jesus Christ done for you personally?

Additional Resources

D. Todd Christofferson, "The Resurrection of Jesus Christ," General Conference, Apr. 2014 (lds.org/general-conference/2014/04/the-resurrection-of-jesus-christ).

"The Living Christ: The Testimony of the Twelve Apostles of The Church of Jesus Christ of Latter-Day Saints," Jan. 1, 2000 (lds.org/bc/content/shared/content/english/pdf/36035_000_25_livingchrist.pdf).

Dieter F. Uchtdorf, "The Hope of God's Light," General Conference, Apr. 2013 (lds.org/general-conference/2013/04/the-hope-of-gods-light).

Memorial Day

Preparation

Find stories about your ancestors (or other people you love who have passed on) that show how the Lord blessed their lives. Some good sources are family members, journals, and your own memories. If you have pioneer ancestors, check out the section devoted to Mormon pioneers on Familysearch.org. Journal entries, news articles, and traveling-company lists of ancestors are automatically identified on your tree. Simply log onto familysearch.org and find the section labeled "Have Pioneer Ancestors?"

Song

"Oh, What Songs of the Heart" (*Hymns*, no. 286)

Lesson

On Memorial Day we honor men and women who died while protecting our country. Many people also reserve the day to remember other loved ones who have passed on. As we think of our forbearers and their trials, we often consider how their sacrifices blessed others. What things do you have to be thankful for because of other people's sacrifices?

Read Alma 36:2–3 to learn what a Book of Mormon prophet says about remembering those who have gone before. Share stories about times when the Lord has blessed and preserved your family members during their trials. How does remembering those who have gone before help us in our trials? What can you learn from their examples?

Read Alma 37:17. As we come to rely on and trust our Heavenly Father and our Savior Jesus Christ, we will realize Their promises to us will always be fulfilled, no matter what comes—even death. In 1 Corinthians 15:55, the Apostle Paul asks, "Oh death where is thy sting? Oh grave where is thy victory?" Because of Jesus Christ, all who have died will be resurrected, and all the Lord's promises to His righteous children can be fulfilled.

Visit a cemetery in your area. If possible, look for your ancestors' graves. You may want to take a few flowers to place on headstones. As you walk through the cemetery, consider the Lord's promise in Doctrine and Covenants 29:26: "But, behold, verily I say unto you, before the earth shall pass away, Michael, mine archangel, shall sound his trump, and then shall all the dead awake, for their graves shall be opened, and they shall come forth—yea, even all."

Additional Resources

William R. Walker, "Live True to the Faith," General Conference, Apr. 2013 (lds.org/general-conference/2014/04/live-true-to-the-faith).

Fourth of July

Preparation

Access the video *Highlight: Loving and Living with Differences,* by Elder Dallin H. Oaks (youtube.com/watch?=MOgQENdDbSs&list=PLClOO0BdaFaNmUqc3ItZJgiuQC9AuoGVo&index=8).

Song

"America the Beautiful" (*Hymns,* no. 338)

Lesson

Name the blessings mentioned in the hymn. In the midst of strife and differing opinions, we often don't see how blessed we are and how miraculous the birth of our country was. Read 2 Nephi 10:10–14. List other blessings you have received because of where you live.

Watch *Highlight: Loving and Living with Differences.* What are some things you can do to follow the counsel of Elder Oaks in your own lives? Buy your favorite kind of ice cream. Go to a park and eat your ice cream as you walk together.

Additional Resources

Dallin H. Oaks, "Loving and Living with Differences," General Conference, Oct. 2014 (lds.org/general-conference/2014/10/loving-others-and-living-with-differences).

Thanksgiving

Preparation

Find a whiteboard, chalkboard, poster, or notebook you and your spouse can see at the same time. You'll also need something to write with. Access the video clip of President Eyring's talk "Oh, Remember, Remember" on lds.org (lds.org/media-library/video/2009-05-22-o-remember-remember).

Song

On This Day of Joy and Gladness" (*Hymns*, no 64)

Lesson

Read Doctrine and Covenants 59:7–21 Together, write down the things the Lord asks us to do in these verses. Then list the blessings He desires to give us.

How can the things we do help us to both receive and recognize the Lord's blessings?

Watch the video clip from President Eyring's talk. As he considered his day, the Spirit helped him to remember blessings he had not recognized in the moment.

How does renewing our covenants each Sunday, fasting, praying, and remembering the Savior allow us to see the hand of God in our lives? Consider the role of the Holy Ghost in helping us recognize our blessings. How does our worthiness allow the Lord to give us both blessings and opportunities to bless others?

Consider these two ways to count your blessings:

- How has the Lord blessed you through someone else?
- How have you been a blessing to someone else by being a part of the Lord's work?

In the coming week, focus on ways you can serve and bless your spouse. Pray for guidance. In return, ask the Lord to help you see the ways your spouse is a blessing in your life. You may want to leave messages of gratitude for your spouse. Record your experiences.

Additional Resources

Thomas S. Monson, "Consider the Blessings," General Conference, Oct. 2012 (lds.org/general-conference/2012/10/consider-the-blessings?lang=eng).

Christmas

Preparation

Locate the story "Christmas Is Christmas" by Sherrie Johnson in the December 1986 *Liahona* (lds.org/liahona/1986/12/christmas-is-christmas). Cut up strips of paper to write on.

Song

Each of you pick a favorite Christmas hymn. Sing both of them.

Lesson

On your strips of paper, write down all the Christmas traditions you can think of—those your family had as you grew up, those your friends or others had, and traditions you want to try. Make it a race to see who can write down the most traditions in two minutes. Put your slips of paper in a bowl or basket.

Read aloud the story "Christmas Is Christmas." Even though this story is about a child, how might it relate to your new family?

Take turns drawing out slips of paper and reading the traditions. Set aside those you want to try this year or in the future. As you think of your new family and the traditions you want to keep or start, remember that the focus of Christmas should be Christ. You might not be able to do everything you did in the past or everything you want to do now. You may face demands from extended family and friends that don't fit with your schedules or needs. It won't always be easy to know what to do or what to say no to, but as you keep Christ as your focus, you will have many wonderful Christmas experiences.

Pick traditions you both feel you have time for this year and write them on the Traditions Tree (see page 119). Put the others you are interested in doing an envelope labeled "Traditions to Try." Next year, decide which traditions worked and which new ones you want to try. It may take a few years to decide on what you like and want to keep, but you will eventually create a new set of traditions that allow your family to stay close to the Savior throughout the holiday season, and all year long.

Additional Resources

"Christmas Traditions of the Seventy," *Liahona,* Dec. 2010 (lds. org/liahona/2010/12/christmas-traditions-of-the-seventy).

"Christmas," Gospel Topics (lds.org/topics/christmas).

Traditions Tree

Enlarge and copy this page, then cut off the instructions.
Write each of your Christmas traditions on a separate line.

Dessert Ideas

- Fresh fruit with yogurt, peanut butter, or caramel for dipping
- Chocolate-chip cookies
- Zucchini or banana bread
- Chocolate no-bake cookies
- Instant pudding on waffles with whipped topping
- Sugar cookies
- Microwave s'mores
- Muffins
- Raw veggies and ranch-dressing dip
- Chocolate- or yogurt-dipped pretzels or strawberries
- Brownies
- Peanut butter bars
- Ice cream sundaes
- Instant pudding pie in pre-made graham-cracker crust
- Homemade milk shakes or smoothies
- Popcorn
- Microwave chocolate cake in a mug
- JELL-O Jigglers
- Cake-mix cookies

Chocolate Peanut Butter No-Bake Cookies

1¾ cups sugar

2 tablespoons baking cocoa

½ cup milk

¼ cup butter

½ teaspoon vanilla

¼ teaspoon salt

½ cup peanut butter

3 cups old-fashioned or quick oats

Heat sugar, cocoa, milk, and butter in a saucepan over medium heat. Boil for one minute, stirring frequently. After one minute, add vanilla and salt. While the other ingredients heat, put the oats and peanut butter in a bowl. Poor chocolate mixture over top; mix well. Drop rounded spoonfuls onto aluminum foil or wax paper. Let cool. Enjoy the cookies as-is, or store them in the refrigerator and eat them cold.

Banana Muffins

4 small, ripe bananas

⅓ cup oil

½ cup sugar

¼ cup honey

1 egg

½ teaspoon vanilla

1 teaspoon baking soda

¼ teaspoon salt

1½ cup whole-wheat or white flour

1 cup nuts or chocolate chips (optional)

Preheat oven to 350°F. Grease a muffin tin or use paper liners. Mash the bananas in a bowl. Mix in oil, sugar, honey, egg, and vanilla. Add baking soda, salt, and flour; combine well. Stir in nuts or chocolate chips (optional). Fill muffin cups. Bake for 20 to 25 minutes or until a toothpick inserted in the center of a muffin comes out clean. Freeze extra muffins for a quick snack later.

Pumpkin Chocolate Chip Cookies

1½ cups sugar

¾ cup shortening or softened butter

1 egg

15-ounce can of pumpkin purée

½ teaspoon salt

1 teaspoon baking soda

1 teaspoon baking powder

3 cups flour

2 tablespoons warm water

1 teaspoon pumpkin-pie spice

1½ cups chocolate chips

Preheat oven to 425°F. Cream together the sugar, shortening, eggs, pumpkin purée, and warm water.

In a separate bowl, mix salt, baking soda, baking powder, flour, and pumpkin-pie spice. Combine flour mixture with other ingredients; mix thoroughly. Stir in chocolate chips. Drop dough by spoonfuls onto a greased cookie sheet. Bake for 9 to 11 minutes.

Brownies

1 cup butter
4 eggs
1 tablespoon vanilla
2 cups sugar
1½ cups flour
½ cup baking cocoa

Preheat oven to 350°F. Grease a 9 x 13-inch pan. Melt butter and set aside to cool. Beat eggs in large bowl. Add remaining ingredients. Pour cooled butter into mixture while stirring. Don't mix too long or it will make the brownies cake-like instead of chewy. Pour into the pan and bake for 30 minutes.

About the Author

JoLyn Brown was raised alongside a peach orchard where she worked with her family. Some of her favorite memories are of listening to stories told by her relatives. These stories and her own experiences provide inspiration for her writing. Her published works include the novel *Run,* several short stories, and *A Circle of Sisters,* an anthology of true stories about the Relief Society. JoLyn is currently working on a romantic fantasy novel and several companion novels to *Run.* She lives in Utah with her husband and two children. When she's not writing, she sews, scrapbooks, reads, and spends time with her family. Learn more about JoLyn and her books by visiting www.jolynbrown.blogspot.com.